FAMOUS ANIMAL STORIES

PLUTO
Brave Lipizzaner Stallion

By Anne Colver

Illustrated by Sam Savitt

Consultant: Rita Grenci   Fox Hill Farm Stables

GARRARD PUBLISHING COMPANY
CHAMPAIGN, ILLINOIS

PLUTO

Brave Lipizzaner Stallion

Young Max Stifel had never run so fast in his life. Up, up the steep mountain path, stumbling over rocks, Max ran on. His breath came in gasps, but he was too excited to stop.

Over his head the early spring sky was blue. The high mountains of the Alps pointed white snow-capped peaks into the clouds. Far below lay the village of St. Martins, where Max lived. His father's farm looked like a small green dot in the valley.

Max looked straight ahead at the gray castle towers halfway up the mountain.

Max had started running the moment he had heard the exciting news in the crowded village market.

A big man had said, "I hear that four young men at the Lipizzaner stable were called to the army. Now they will be hiring some of our younger boys to work with the horses."

Max knew that the man meant the Lipizzaner stallions, the most famous horses in Austria—maybe in the whole world. He knew the Lipizzaners had been brought from the Palace Stables in the city of Vienna to escape the bombings of the long war in Europe. They were safe in the stables of the old castle.

Max touched the big man's arm. "Excuse me, Herr Grotte. What boys will they hire?"

Max was surprised to hear himself speak, for he was a shy boy.

The big man answered, "The ones who get there first."

Max ran through the stone gates of the castle to the stable door and stopped.

He had nearly bumped into a gray-haired man in army uniform.

"Oh—" Max tried to catch his breath. "Excuse me, sir, I—was running—"

"So I see." The man's blue eyes were not unkind. "If you have come about work—"

"Oh, yes, sir." Max nodded hard. He breathed the exciting stable smell of horses, leather, and fresh hay. Beyond the man's shoulder he could see the long lines of stalls. In each stall stood one of the white stallions. Over each stall door was one of the famous names: FAVORY, NEAPOLITANO. Max knew them all by heart, but he was looking for one special name—PLUTO, the famous leader of the

Lipizzaners. Everyone had heard stories of Pluto's bravery. Max saw the name at last. PLUTO. Then he saw the white stallion's beautiful head.

The man's voice cut in. "How old are you?"

"Fourteen my next birthday, sir." Max did not add that his thirteenth birthday had been last week.

"You are too young," he said. "And I have already hired the boys we—"

A sudden loud whinny from the back of the stable cut the words short. The whinny was followed by snorting and kicking and a voice shouting, "Get away from Pluto. Get out *now!*"

Max saw a tall man striding past the stalls toward them. He also

wore the uniform of an army officer. The heels of his high polished boots clicked on the floor.

"Josef! Do you see this?" The tall officer held out a stick to the gray-haired man. "I just saw one of the· boys you hired whipping Pluto with this stick. He said Pluto wouldn't move out of his way while he swept the stall."

Josef's face was red. "I am very sorry, colonel."

Max suddenly knew that the tall officer was Colonel Podhajsky, Herr Director of the Lipizzaner stallions.

The colonel went on angrily. "You know, Josef, that I never allow a whip on one of my horses. They are trained with skill and much patience, but they never feel a whip." He broke the stick over his knee. "I have sent the boy away. Now find me another."

8

The colonel turned and seemed to see Max for the first time. "Who are you?" he asked.

Max wasn't sure whether he should salute the colonel. This time he *mustn't* be shy, he thought. He made a little bow and tried to click his heels. "My name is Max Stifel, Herr Colonel. My father has a farm near the village. I came here hoping to work with the Lipizzaners."

The colonel looked at Max. "Max, would you ever whip a horse?"

"Oh, no! Our old horse, Dopple, works my father's farm. Sometimes he does not want to move. But if anyone whipped Dopple my father would be just as—as angry—as angry as you are now, Herr Colonel."

Colonel Podhajsky turned toward Herr Josef. "I think this boy understands horses. Put him to work tomorrow and teach him yourself."

That night Max was too excited to sleep. Tomorrow he would be working in the Lipizzaner stables. Perhaps he would even have a chance to take care of Pluto. Perhaps being brave was catching, like measles. Being near the brave Pluto might help.

The first days of working at the castle stables were hard. Max carried wood for the stoves, washed windows, unloaded hay. He had been close to the horses only a few times, when Herr Josef told him to sweep stalls. But he was never told to sweep Pluto's stall. Max could only steal a quick look now and then at the great stallion. Once Pluto looked back as Max passed the stall. Max put out his hand and touched the horse's white neck. "Pluto," he whispered. He

saw Herr Josef watching and hurried on with his work.

Any boy in Austria would be proud to work with the famous white stallions. The first Lipizzaner horses had been brought from Spain by the Austrian Archduke Charles. The emperor himself had ridden one of the first Lipizzaner stallions. He built stables for the horses across the Palace courtyard and a great hall where the horses could perform for the emperor and his royal visitors.

Each new generation of Lipizzaners had been carefully bred and trained to perform graceful jumps and complicated paces.

One afternoon Max learned more. It was pouring rain outside. "We will work indoors and polish harness," Herr Josef told the stable boys.

Max worked with the others, rubbing

oil on leather bridles and heavy saddles, shining brass buckles. He loved the smell of leather and horses.

In an unusually friendly mood, Herr Josef sat with the boys by the stove and told them stories as he puffed on his pipe. He told about performances of the Lipizzaners in the Palace Hall in Vienna.

"The hall was all white and scarlet,"

Herr Josef said. "The lights sparkled as if they were diamonds. Our horses were beautiful. Each one went through his difficult paces. They even danced to the music—"

Max interrupted eagerly. "I know. I have watched the horses exercise in the yard. I know the wonderful way they jump with four feet in the air and walk on their hind legs and—"

Herr Josef frowned. "The horses you see are playing at tricks," he said. "We have only six riders here, and they are too old for army service. They cannot train all our horses as true Lipizzaners are trained. And we have no Palace Hall, no lights, no music, no audiences."

"But I have seen Pluto—" Max said.

"Pluto is different." Herr Josef's voice softened. "Colonel Podhajsky rides and trains him every day. Only Pluto remembers his difficult steps. When the war ends and the Lipizzaners can go back to Vienna, Pluto will still lead them as he did during the terrible bombing."

The boys listened as Herr Josef told the exciting story of how Pluto had saved the other stallions. "The bombs were falling all over the city. A corner of our stable was hit. We tried to lead the horses to a bomb shelter in the Palace. But they were too frightened to move until the colonel walked Pluto slowly past each stall. Even with bombs crashing, Pluto walked quietly. And the other horses followed him, one by one, across the courtyard into the shelter. Only Blitzen was left in the stables."

"But why?" one of the boys asked.

"Blitzen is our youngest stallion," Herr Josef said. "He is a beautiful horse, and he performs brilliantly. But he is shy,

and nervous. When the colonel saw that Blitzen had not come with the others, he took Pluto back across the open courtyard once again. Pluto stood by Blitzen's stall until Blitzen was quiet enough to follow. At the stable door a bomb exploded almost in their faces, but Pluto stayed close by Blitzen and led him across safely."

Before Max left the stable that evening, he went into Blitzen's stall. "You and I know what it feels like to be shy," Max said. The stallion pricked his small ears. Max rubbed one ear and laughed. "You Lipizzaners have such little ears—but you hear everything."

When Max was through with school for the year, he worked at the stable all day. Herr Josef let him work more with the horses. Max often led one of the stallions on a long rein to exercise in the stable yard. But never Pluto.

One morning Max was surprised when Herr Josef met him at the door.

"I'm glad to see you, Max," Herr Josef said. "Two of the stable boys are sick. The colonel sent four men with trucks to bring hay for the horses. They should have come back last night. But there has been no word from them. We'll have to manage somehow."

He tossed Max a pitchfork. "Start cleaning. Take Pluto's stall first."

Max walked into Pluto's stall. He had wondered a hundred times what it would be like really to be near Pluto. Now he put his hand on the stallion's white neck and said softly, "Pluto."

The big stallion pricked his ears and turned to look at Max. Max found himself looking back into brown eyes so dark they seemed almost purple. He had never seen eyes so gentle. He had never felt a horse as quiet under his hand. And yet Pluto was the leader of the Lipizzaners. He had been brave enough to save the others from the bombed stables in Vienna. "What is your secret of being brave?" Max wondered.

For a moment longer the horse and the boy looked at each other.

Then Max began to work. He was halfway down the line of stalls when Herr Josef came toward him, frowning. "Our trucks are still not back. The colonel is worried. The war news on the radio is bad."

Suddenly there was a flash of lightning and a crash of thunder. The sky was black.

"It's one of our mountain storms," Max said. "A bad one."

The horses were already excited. They stamped and shook their heads.

"It sounds like the bombings," Herr Josef said. "They are badly frightened."

Suddenly Colonel Podhajsky was there. Then came another split of lightning. "Get to the horses," the colonel called. "Try to quiet them."

With each loud clap of thunder, the horses kicked and snorted. Max stopped at the first stalls, touching the horses, trying to speak quietly. Then there was a sound of splintering wood, and Max saw Blitzen kicking his stall. The young stallion's eyes were wild with fear.

Max ran to the stall. There was blood on the horse's leg. Blitzen had kicked through the wall. Max knew that he must keep Blitzen away from the jagged, splintered hole. As he pushed the horse away to the other side of the stall, one flying kick caught Max's leg. He felt a stab of pain.

"Quiet, Blitzen," Max coaxed. "It's all right." His hand was still on Blitzen's neck when the storm finally rolled past.

Colonel Podhajsky came into the stall. He bandaged Blitzen's bloody leg. "Just a small cut," the colonel said to Max. "You saved him from breaking his leg. Talking to him is the best way to handle a horse like Blitzen. You know how to talk to him, Max. It could have been much worse."

Max was halfway down the mountain path when he had a surprising thought. Today was the first time he had not been afraid of a thunderstorm.

The next morning Max limped as he went through the castle gate. He saw that the trucks had pulled in, and the four men were talking to Colonel Podhajsky.

"They say the war is ended," the men explained. "Our country has lost, so we will be occupied by American army troops. Tanks and trucks are already rolling in. All roads have been cut off. We could not bring back any hay."

Now everyone was talking at once. Max heard the colonel say, "We have only one day's feed left. Without hay my horses will starve."

"Excuse me, Herr Colonel," Max said, stepping forward. "My father is a farmer. He knows the other farmers in the valley. I think, sir, they will all want to bring hay for the Lipizzaners. I can go and ask my father now."

By afternoon farm wagons were bumping up the mountain road with loads of hay. Max watched as his father drove old Dopple to the stable door. Just then Colonel Podhajsky came riding up on

Pluto. "My Lipizzaners thank you for feeding them," the colonel said to all the farmers. He touched the rein lightly, and Pluto bowed to show his thanks.

The colonel dismounted. "Now I want to thank you myself." He handed Pluto's reins to Max. "Which driver is your father, Max?"

Max pointed. "And that is our Dopple, Herr Colonel."

The colonel went around shaking hands with the farmers. He stopped to rub Dopple's gray nose. "He has a good head," the colonel said.

Max stood holding Pluto. He saw his father beam with pride.

The next morning everyone in St. Martins was awake long before daylight. They gathered in the village square. There was no talk and gossip.

Max stood by his father. He wondered what it would be like to have a strange army take over the country.

Just at dawn jeeps roared into town and stopped at the market place. Young American soldiers jumped out. The soldiers looked around at the people. The people of St. Martins looked back. The square was very silent. The hens in their coops seemed to stop clucking.

One soldier started to read from a paper. The people could not understand what he read.

Max had learned a little English in school. He heard the soldier say, *"All horses will be taken by the army unless they are needed for farm work."*

Max raced from the square. He must warn the colonel.

An army jeep was already at the door

of the stable. An American officer was questioning the colonel. "You have horses stabled here?"

"We have," the colonel said.

"I have an order to take all horses not being used on farms. Your horses must be taken."

"You do not understand." The colonel's face was white and set. "These are the Lipizzaner horses. They are the pride of our country. They are famous all over the world."

The young officer looked up at him. "The Lipizzaners?" It seemed that he remembered something. "Have you a horse here named Pluto?"

"Pluto is the great leader of our Lipizzaners."

"I've heard General Patton talk about Pluto. The general is in command of this section. He is a great horseman.

I think he would want to help your Lipizzaners. I'll try to get a message to him."

An answer from General Patton came the next morning. Colonel Podhajsky read it to the others. "General Patton will be pleased to visit your stables. He greatly admires the Lipizzaners, especially the famous Pluto. He will discuss providing food and protection for the Lipizzaners during the American occupation."

A burst of applause interrupted.

The colonel held up a hand. "Wait! There is more." The colonel continued to read the general's words. "I have never seen the Lipizzaners perform. Therefore, I shall come to the castle with staff and troops on Thursday at noon. We look forward to the performance."

The colonel paused. Then he said, "This is Monday noon. We have three days to prepare a performance for the general."

Max felt the silence around him. Herr Josef exploded, *"Impossible!* The horses have had no training in months. We have no grandstand—no music—only an empty stable yard!"

"It's not impossible, Josef," the colonel answered. "We will begin work at once. Hans will visit the village mayor. The mayor will want St. Martins to welcome the American general properly. He will send carpenters to build a grandstand for the general and his staff. He will see that flags are placed. He will be sure that there is music for the horses to dance to."

"Josef," the colonel went on, "you and the boys will have the saddles and bridles ready for the horses and uniforms ready for our riders."

The colonel finished. "Leave the performance of the horses to Pluto and to me. Pluto will help me teach them what they have forgotten. Our Lipizzaners will be ready."

Max and the other boys helped Herr Josef open the old trunks from Vienna. Max blinked in wonder when he shook out red velvet saddle cloths embroidered in gold. He lifted out saddles and bridles of leather and silver.

Max could imagine how proud the white stallions must have looked when they performed in the Palace Hall.

"Max, Felix, I will need you later," Josef said. "The colonel is using every man who can ride for the performance. There are not enough trained riders for every horse. Some of you boys will have to take horses on lead lines." Herr Josef handed out the long reins.

"Felix, you take Donner. He tries to please. Max, you will take Blitzen. You talked him through the thunderstorm, now talk him through this. He trusts your voice. If you can keep him calm, he will perform magnificently."

Max could not believe he had been chosen. He took the rein as if it were made of gold.

"Now get your horses out to the stable yard. Keep your lines loose. But be sure your horse is under control. Follow the colonel's orders."

Max led Blitzen out. The big stallion walked beside him. "Maybe Blitzen knows how scared I am," Max thought.

"First I will put Pluto through a full performance," Colonel Podhajsky said. "Then he will lead each horse through the moves." He gave a light touch of his heel, and Pluto trotted out.

Max knew the names of the different paces and moves. For the first time he saw each one done perfectly by Pluto.

Pluto led the other stallions, one by one, through the difficult moves. They followed Pluto and remembered their old performances. They paced and trotted with legs high. They jumped off the ground with all four feet and stood on their hind legs.

When it was Blitzen's turn to follow Pluto, Max gripped the long rein. He was surprised how easily the young horse performed. He followed Pluto's every move. As Max led him off the field, he heard the colonel's "Bravo Blitzen."

When the horses had finished, the colonel said, "Of course, the general will expect us to finish with the Grand Quadrille, where the horses perform together. It is the most difficult—and it

must be perfectly done. But they must have music to step to. We will wait until morning."

The next morning the mayor of St. Martins sent the village band. He sent wagon loads of lumber and carpenters to build a stand for the general. He sent flags and bunting to put around the stable yard. The mayor's wife promised refreshments for everyone.

The band struck up as Max watched from the sidelines.

The colonel rode out on Pluto, and the other stallions and riders followed. The horses stepped together to the music in the difficult quadrille. They moved uncertainly at first. But Pluto led them patiently, step by step, again and again, until they moved in perfect time to the music.

After it was over, Colonel Podhajsky

patted Pluto's neck. "Good work, my friend," he said. Then he called to the musicians, "Now play a waltz."

The band swung into a waltz tune. Pluto moved forward, his steps in waltz time. One by one the other horses followed.

Herr Josef looked astonished.

Even the carpenters stopped hammering to watch. The performance was perfect.

By evening a flag-draped stand was ready for the American general.

"We have a performance ready for tomorrow," Colonel Podhajsky said. "Pray for good weather."

That night Max prayed hard for good weather. Then he added, "And please let Blitzen do well."

The next morning Max walked into the stable before daylight. The uniform

Herr Josef had loaned him hung carefully over his arm. His mother had pressed the white trousers and brown coat. Max had polished the borrowed boots and stuffed the toes with paper to make them fit. He held his black cap.

Herr Josef was waiting. "The colonel wants a last rehearsal," he told the boys. "Groom your horses. Be sure to oil their hooves. Brush their manes and tails. Then put on your uniforms."

They hurried to obey. The whole stable seemed to be charged with electricity. Blitzen looked around nervously whenever Max touched him. Everyone talked in whispers.

Only Pluto, in his stall, looked calmly out of his velvety brown-purple eyes.

Horses and riders were in the stable yard by daybreak. Max held Blitzen's long rein.

For a long minute, before the last practice started, everyone stopped to watch the great golden sun rise behind the mountain peaks into a clear sky.

"It will be a good day," Herr Josef breathed in relief.

Max's first prayer had been answered. He hoped God would not forget his second one. *"Please* let Blitzen do well."

"Now let us get on with the rehearsal," the colonel said.

Before noon, horses and riders were back in the stable. Every horse was saddled and bridled. Every rider had given his high boots a last gleaming polish, straightened his hat, and squared his shoulders.

Max stood by Blitzen. He heard the village clock wheeze out a count of twelve. At the last stroke a parade of jeeps roared up to the stable. Max

watched through the door and saw the
American General Patton step out of his
jeep. He saw Colonel Podhajsky and the
general exchange salutes. "I greet you,
sir," the colonel said. Then he brought
Pluto to the general. "Pluto greets you
for the Lipizzaners."

The mayor bowed deeply to the
general. His face shone as brightly as
the medals that covered his jacket as he
led the guests proudly to the flag-draped

stand of honor. A long line of soldiers came next. They were followed by the villagers, dressed in their best, who had come to see the show.

The band burst into a loud *oom-pah*.

At the sudden noise Blitzen laid back his ears and pulled on the rein. Max coaxed him gently. "Remember, Blitzen, today we must both be brave." He gently patted the stallion's neck.

The performance had begun outside.

Through the stable door Max watched the beautiful stallion Favory finish with a brilliant *capriole*. The big horse leaped with four feet flying above the ground. One after another the stallions performed. The audience was delighted. Max could peek around the door at General Patton. He looked pleased.

Then it was Pluto's turn. The audience watched spellbound.

Herr Josef came by Max. "You boys will be on after Pluto. Have your horses ready," he said. "Felix, straighten your cap. Hans, remember to pick up your feet. Max, keep your horse more quiet."

The boys led their horses into the yard just as Pluto finished his final *courbette*. The great stallion rose and walked lightly on his hind legs, turning in time to the music. The colonel rode off the field to a storm of applause.

Max looked anxiously at Blitzen. The young horse stood steadily.

Max felt as though he were dreaming as he led Blitzen out. He knew the crowd was there. He saw the flags. He heard the music. His hand was tight on the rein. He was ready.

But the audience was still clapping for Pluto. Max saw the colonel ride Pluto back to make a last bow. Suddenly the crowd was stamping and shouting. Max felt Blitzen tremble. Someone waved a handkerchief in Blitzen's face.

Blitzen reared in terror. Max tried desperately. "Quiet, Blitzen. Please, Blitzen, *please*—"

It was no use. In a horrified moment Max knew that Blitzen was out of control. Herr Josef, red-faced, ran toward him. Herr Josef would take the rein and lead Blitzen off the field in disgrace.

Max felt sudden tears in his eyes. "I'm sorry, Blitzen." Then, through the tears, he saw a horse with gentle, purple-brown eyes between him and Herr Josef's angry face. Colonel Podhajsky had brought Pluto back to help.

Pluto stood quietly beside the very frightened young stallion. Max could feel Blitzen's trembling stop.

The band still played. The audience waited.

The colonel touched his heel lightly. Pluto took a careful step, then another.

Blitzen hesitated. Max pulled the rein gently. Blitzen moved forward and began his paces. Max moved beside him, as if he were part of the horse. Blitzen performed without a mistake.

"Good Blitzen," Max said. His part was finished. Back in the stall, he rubbed down his horse and said over and over, "Good Blitzen. I was very proud. You are a wonderful performer."

Max went back to the field to watch the last of the Grand Quadrille. The line of stallions moved perfectly together, following Pluto without a mistake. At the end there was a last thunder of applause and shouts. Max was thankful that Blitzen was safely back in the stall eating his measure of oats.

Minutes later the news flew around the stables.

General Patton had promised that the Lipizzaners would be protected until it was safe to take them back to Vienna. The performance had been a success!

Max heard the news with joy. Pluto had saved the Lipizzaners once more. Then he thought, "When they go back to Vienna, I will never see them again."

Photo Credits:
Top left: Wide World Photos
Left: Wide World Photos
Above: Pictorial Parade Inc.
Right: United Press International

THE LIPIZZANERS PERFORM

Max was bedding Blitzen with fresh straw when Colonel Podhajsky stopped by the stall. "You did well with your horse this afternoon, Max. We will be leaving St. Martins soon, but perhaps someday you will come to Vienna. If you do, you will find work with the Lipizzaners."

Max looked up at the stars that night. Had he learned Pluto's secret of being brave? He remembered the moment on the field when Blitzen had almost bolted. Max hadn't been worried about himself— he only wanted to help Blitzen. Perhaps he had learned a little. Perhaps he would learn more.

The stars were still shining when Max fell asleep.